Praise for A to Z

Excerpts from Amazon Reviews:

"You know you are in good hands while working through this beautifully written and well thought out book. Don't just read the book and move on, I urge you to take out your pen and paper and get to work." *Annie*

"It is very relevant to my life at this juncture and helped me to realize that a new career path was still a viable possibility for me, as long as I was willing to make the effort to truly define my new goals through personal introspection, as outlined in Diane's book." *Linda*

"A to Z will capture your attention and get you thinking. It's short and to the point, so it's easy to read, which is important, since you will want to read it more than once." *Joslyn*

"Diane's new book is both refreshing and energizing in helping to gain clarity about what the cornerstone of an inspired life and career could be." *Bryan*

"The A to Z format offers bite-sized encouragement to help you dig deep and discover what you really want. Highly recommended." *PR*

"Diane's book is an amazing guide to thinking about what you want out of this life. Diane uses pertinent quotes, her own experience and the experiences of her clients to coach your thinking strategies." *Glenda*

"This is a very relevant topic for so many people who are finding themselves in the position of looking for a new career, whether it is by one's own choosing or not. *Jayne*

Loved reading Diane's book, she's so insightful and encouraging. This is a must read for anyone entering this stage of their life." *Chris*

A to Z:

26 Keys

to

Unlock Career
Change Success

for

Midlife Women

Diane Howell Topkis

Original Kindle cover by pro_ebookcovers

ISBN: 978-0-9967661-3-5 (paperback)

ASIN: B00NVHOS2U (ebook)

Terre Ventures Publishing

Printed by CreateSpace, An Amazon.com Company

Printed in the United States of America

*Dedicated to all midlife women
searching for a
more meaningful next chapter.*

Table of Contents

To My Reader

THIS BOOK IS WRITTEN FOR MIDLIFE WOMEN (and enlightened men) who are looking for something more meaningful from their careers. I share 26 key elements necessary to start you on your midlife career transition. These keys are based on my own experiences as well as perspectives gleaned from my career coaching clients. I know they work.

I saw how clients came to coaching—the issues, concerns, not knowing where to start. After our work together, the clarity and confidence they gained allowed them to get unstuck, make more conscious choices, and move forward. Now I'm sharing them with you to help you move forward toward your dreams.

I'm assuming you picked up this book because like my clients, you're in midlife and at a crossroad in your career. You're dissatisfied and searching for an alternative. If you're feeling that something is missing in your work, read on, this book is for you.

Beware. This book is not about your job search. It's about finding out who you are, your values, your inner drive—all of which must come before what you do and how you do it. Once you have this clarity, you will naturally have the confidence to discover new possibilities and reach new levels of personal and professional success.

What's the message behind the book?

YOU'LL LEARN THAT THE SECRET to success is deceptively simple—unlock your truest self and align your career to it. I'll admit, that's a lot easier said than done. Working through these keys will lay the groundwork for your personal platform for success, based on your authentic self. You'll discover a more direct connection with your power, strength, and wisdom. I guarantee the knowledge you gain about yourself will change the way you look at your world forever.

As a career coach for midlife women, I have seen these keys work. I've heard the surprise and joy as clients discover their authentic self. Often it's the first time they clearly understand their value, what they're all about, and can express what they really want. And that gives them the confidence to go get it.

With the right mindset, self-knowledge, and awareness, you can realize the full potential of your life. Yes, you may be dissatisfied with your career but midlife is not so much about just finding a new job. It's more a matter of becoming who you were meant to be. Only then can reinventing or re-energizing your career be successful. My hope is that you discover your passion, become intentional about your career, and do work you love.

Throughout this book you will see the icon of my business, a dragonfly. It is said to symbolize the subconscious or the dreaming mind. They ask us to be more aware of our deepest thoughts and desires to let our inner light shine through with a new vision and clarity. I wish that for you. I hope my book helps.

How is this book different?

THERE ARE HUNDREDS OF CAREER BOOKS but not all are pertinent to midlife and beyond. It's by no means exhaustive information on each key. It's meant to start you thinking—understanding where you are now, where you need to focus, and go deeper to find out *who* you are—all of which must come before the job search. You must first look inward so you can align your work with who you are.

My wish is that you find *A to Z* helpful and filled with strategies you can put to use right away. Read it sequentially cover to cover or skip around the alphabet. Give yourself time to absorb each key. Be sure to work through the posed questions but don't stop at your first answer. Dig deeper.

Some keys may seem obvious. If that happens just ask yourself—have I *really* focused on this? Most people have not. Use these keys to identify your own personal keys to stay ahead of others in the workplace.

If I can encourage and inspire you to reach for something more in your work life, then I've done my job. You picked up this book for a reason. Embrace that reason. Roll up your sleeves and do the work. Find out who you are—and then find the career to align with it. I'm confident you can do it.

Although this was written based on my work with midlife women, I encourage enlightened midlife men to read it as well. All these concepts easily fit men looking for more meaningful work.

This is the introductory book of my Career Clarity series. Stay tuned for more. All are based on my CLEAR Path signature coaching process. If you can't wait to get started, check out my coaching programs at and download my free workbook, *Find Your Career Passion* at http://www.YourNextChapterNOW.com.

Let's Begin

MIDLIFE SHIFTS OUR FOCUS to our unexplored potential, to find our inner drive, and discover our true path. How can we navigate this complex and often uncharted territory? In a culture that thrives on instant gratification, the answers do not come quickly or easily. The reflection and questioning process takes patience, persistence, and a good deal of courage.

There are so many feelings and thoughts that go through our minds as we enter midlife, let alone assessing where we are in our careers. The second time I said, "It runs the gamut from A to Z," I realized that I wanted to organize my thinking around the alphabet. This book is a combination of finding out who we are and what we need to be successful at this stage of life in order to live our next chapter in a more purposeful and meaningful way.

Picking the right words for each letter was an interesting and fun process. So many words could have fit midlife, and lots for career, and of course, for women. My challenge was to blend them together into what is important for midlife women.

You'll find many connections between the letters but they all start with the first entry—*Authentic.* This is what midlife is all about—finally knowing who you are, and what you want and need in your life and career.

A number or surveys and articles tell us the midlife woman views this life stage as a time to reinvent herself—to do all the things she never had time for—to take care of herself both inside and out. This is your time. If not now, when? There's an urgency at this stage of life to find a clear path to your next chapter.

To discover yourself in midlife may require you to go through some difficult moments as you dig deep for answers. Scott Peck, the author of *The Road Less Traveled,* said that, "The truth is that our finest moments are most likely to occur when we are feeling deeply uncomfortable, unhappy, or unfulfilled. For it is only in such moments, propelled by our discomfort, that we are likely to step out of our ruts and start searching for different ways or truer answers."

I am honored to be part of your adventure.

Authentic

THERE'S AN ACUTE AWAKENING to authenticity in midlife. It's a time of transition when we have the opportunity to create a life and career around our true self, living consciously, and with intent. To live authentically you must seek the truth of who you are. To access that truth, you listen to your heart and to your inner voice.

When you fashion a life where the decisions you make and the actions you take are considered, deliberate, and in harmony with what's important to you, you are living an authentic life. It's not necessarily a life that others admire or think is right for you, but a life that you know in your heart is right.

I personally believe there is nothing more important than honoring your authentic self, your true nature, and expressing it in the world. When you honor yourself, you allow your light to shine. It's your gift to the world.

When we were younger, we were often focused on pleasing others—parents, teachers, bosses, and spouses. We learned to play by other people's rules. As we mature into midlife, we become more competent, independent, and are less motivated to do what others want us to do.

It starts with knowing who you are and what your truth is. The more honest you can be, with yourself and with others, about who you are and what you need to be fulfilled, the more likely you are to create a life that's right for you. However, excavating your truth may seem like a daunting task.

So, how do you go about showing the world who you really are? Start by accepting yourself as you are right now. Own your story. Stop worrying about who you think you should be. Be compassionate. Embrace yourself. Living your truth starts with being honest with yourself, acknowledging, and accepting what you are feeling. Sit with that emotion, feel it in your body, and in your heart. Know what is real and true for you. Once you know your truth, it will be easier to communicate it to others.

Once you know and accept who you are, suddenly some areas of your life may not feel aligned. Often that's your career. This is the time for your authentic career—the one that honors your essential self. The one just for you—not the one you pursued because you were "supposed" to. Perhaps you began your career with great hope and ambition, but after a while it turned out to be a grind. Doing the same thing day after day without paying attention to your authentic self can drain your energy and enthusiasm. You lose your creative spark.

Perhaps your career didn't lead you to where you wanted to go. Or you may be a big success at what you do but no longer feel passionate about it. Whichever it is, you know deep from within, it's time for a change. Now is your chance to truly understand yourself and what would satisfy you. It's time to learn about your own needs and desires, and craft the career that fits you.

Living authentically is not always easy. It can require courage to continue your path regardless of the opinions and beliefs of others. However, once you are clear about what resonates for you, and you align your outer behavior with that inner truth, your life will flow in a direction that is exquisitely meaningful.

"To thine own self be true."
~ William Shakespeare ~

Brand

BRAND YOU, YOU INC., or the CEO of you. Whatever it's been called over the years, it all comes down to that fact that *you* are in control of how you are perceived, and what you represent in the marketplace. The only problem is that most of us haven't put it all together, let alone manage it.

A brand is a promise. Think of well-known product brands like Nike or Apple, or your own favorite local spa. You repeatedly buy because they're consistent. They stand for something in your mind.

It's the same idea for a person. Next time someone walks into the office or approaches you, what's your immediate thought about them? Whether good or not so good, that's part of their brand. Even if it's a thought about how they dress.

Or let's try someone more obvious like Oprah. At the time of this writing, she's #14 on Fortune's Most Powerful Women list. Talk about a strong personal brand! And she certainly defines having a meaningful career.

As she headed to her next chapter, David Zaslav talked her into a 50/50 partnership for a new cable network, OWN—Oprah Winfrey Network. He didn't want her money. He wanted her name and time. She worried about losing her authentic self. Part of her own growth was accepting that even being a brand, she could stay true to herself and her viewers.

By midlife, whether you realize it or not, you have spent many years of your career developing your personal brand. Your values, your skills, and talents all contribute to your brand. How do others perceive you? Is that the message you want to send out? What do you stand for? What do you consistently deliver? How do you want people to feel when they interact with you? Name 3 adjectives you want to be known for.

If you want to advance your career, no matter if in your current one or something new, these are questions you must be able to answer. And be able to consistently communicate it in a concise, clear manner so your audience understands your value. Then you must manage your brand in everything you do.

Branding is the business of being you. Your personal brand—the value that others perceive you possess—is something you can and must develop, shape, and control. It's what makes you unique—and better than all of your competition.

"Your brand is what people say about you
when you're not in the room."
~ Jeff Bezos ~

Clarity

THERE ARE SO MANY C WORDS that fit; I didn't think I could choose just one until I decided on "clarity" because the midlife woman's search for clarity is the basis of everything. At this time of life, we shed our desire to always please others. Being clear about who you are and what you want is very powerful. Anything can happen!

Gaining clarity is a process, like peeling an onion (hopefully without all the tears). There are many layers of clarity to strive for but the most important, at the core, is who you are and what you stand for. Everything else falls into place from there.

How to get clear? First, start very simply. Find quiet time to think and dream. Sharpen your awareness of what's going on in and around you to begin to understand what gives you pleasure and satisfaction in your life—and the opposite. Do something mindless. Let your thoughts float freely. When was a time you felt great? What were you doing? Who were you with? These are the starting clues to your future vision.

My coaching clients spend several sessions exploring their values, skills, and talents, narrowing them down to their essential drivers. This is always their "aha" moment. We midlife women rarely spend time learning about ourselves at this deep level. This is who you are. Everything starts to make sense. We now have a clearer view of why something isn't working and what we need in our life.

As the song lyrics go "on a clear day you can see forever." Now that you know what drives you and who you are, look into the future for your life and career. Envision how you want it to be, so you can make it so.

Clarity is the catalyst to action. With clarity comes confidence. When you're confident and committed, action takes surprisingly little effort because decision making becomes easier.

Be sure you are clear on what *you* want. It probably won't fit anyone else. Another's midlife reinvention may sound good but it may not be right for you. Don't copy. Instead, let it be an inspiration to find your own reinvention. And if you're passionate about something the rest of your world doesn't agree with, still go for it. It's your passion not theirs. Go for it, even if you don't think you have a chance.

Clarity leads to confidence which leads to conscious and easier choices—in your career and life.

"Clarity is the most important thing. I can compare clarity to pruning in gardening. You know you need to be clear. If you are not clear, nothing is going to happen. You have to be clear. Then you have to be confident about your vision. And after that, you just have to put a lot of work in."
~ Diane von Furstenberg ~

Daring

DARING GREATLY. Brene Brown brought this phrase to the attention of a wide audience through her 2010 TED talk. The phrasing came from a quote by Theodore Roosevelt commonly referred to as The Man in the Arena speech:

"It is not the critic who counts...credit belongs to the man who is actually in the arena...who at the worst, if he fails, at least fails while daring greatly."

Brown likened this to her studies on vulnerability. It's not about knowing victory or defeat. It's understanding that both are needed to be fully engaged. It's being all in. She says our willingness to own and engage with our vulnerability determines the depth of our courage and clarity of purpose. "We must walk into the arena with courage and willingness to engage. We must dare to show up and let ourselves be seen. This is vulnerability. This is daring greatly."

This is midlife. If we want to move forward, claim our authentic self, we need to allow ourselves to become more vulnerable, and step into the arena.

Before "daring greatly" became the cool phrase, I called this "stretching," the act of doing something you know is good for you yet it scares you because you are moving out of your comfort zone. Think of that nice comfy bubble around you. You can relax staying within your boundaries, but it can also be a boring place to hide.

If you are going to do serious self-inquiry and do it truthfully, you will definitely be daring greatly, and moving out of your comfort zone. You will be asking yourself tough questions that may not be easy to answer. But each little stretch makes you more resilient and stronger.

Your comfort zone will expand and become your power zone. The larger it becomes the more power you have. The more you can handle. The wider your zone, the richer your life becomes. Along with it comes greater self-confidence, self-trust, and helps you grow even further.

Stretching the edges of your comfort zone is always going to be uncomfortable but how else will you know that you are moving to the next level? Are you ready to dare greatly?

"Vulnerability is the birthplace of love, belonging,
joy, courage, empathy, and creativity.
It is the source of hope, empathy, accountability,
and authenticity. If we want greater clarity in
our purpose or deeper and
more meaningful spiritual lives,
vulnerability is the path."
~ Brene Brown ~

Energy

ENERGY IS LIFE. It's the power deep inside that drives you. It gives form to your deepest feelings and passions—to who you are and what you can become.

Energy is that spark that ignites when you have a special connection. Whether it's with another human being, a thing of beauty like a sunset or music, or with something that enlarges your world, it changes the way you see or feel. It's also the way you feel when your career is really on. When the sparks fly and you just love what you do.

Change takes energy. So, how do we generate the energy needed for transformation? First, be physically strong. Eat correctly. Exercise. If you hate the gym, take walks, anything to get moving.

I've chosen to develop a yoga practice, expecting the calming results, but was surprised at getting a stronger body. Being healthy physically helps fuel the energy needed to be psychologically strong. You know the adage—strong body, strong mind.

Next, release negative energy. Unfortunately, we all have destructive energy around us. Buried energy, long suppressed, held inside, weighing us down. At midlife, it's high time we rid ourselves of what drains us. Free yourself from toxic relationships, unfound worries, and anything that drains your focus.

Like energy attracts like energy. If your focus stays on the negative, more negative will come to you. Try this: divide your relationships and your environment into 2 lists – Energy Drains and Energy Sparks. Now list the impact each has on you.

Eliminating the Drains will free up more energy for you than simply adding more Sparks. Make a conscious choice to move away from the Drains. You can do it. You just have to be motivated. Be strong.

Now there's room to generate positive energy. As we begin to nurture and consciously care for the energy in our life, we come alive and bring emotional depth and authenticity, spontaneity, and joy into our world.

Most important, be clear on your future vision and why. If you understand your motivation and reasons for changing, your energy and enthusiasm will naturally be high. Your motivation is what will help you build your plan and work it through until you reach your dream.

"Passion is energy. Feel the power that comes from focusing on what excites you."
~ Oprah Winfrey ~

Flâneur

ISN'T THAT A FABULOUS WORD? Flâneur has no direct translation to English but in French it means "stroller, saunterer." The French poet, Charles Baudelaire defined flâneur as that of "a person who walks the city in order to experience it." My version is "a person who strolls through life in order to experience it."

However, being a flâneuse (the feminine version) is not about being slow and aimless. It's about your willingness to be open. With eyes open you follow your path, allowing for serendipity (another of my favorite words). Be interested and inquisitive. Be inspired. Take in other people, other ideas. Ask lots of questions. Find unexpected encounters and connections.

An apt adage, "All work and no play makes Jane a dull girl." You may have to loosen up your tightly scheduled calendar to allow a little wandering time.

Do you take the same route home, go to the same coffee shop, same...whatever? Change it up a bit. Start simply. Take a different route home or to the office. You know those side streets that you zoom past? Take one or two turns, check them out. Go the local route. Look around.

I hope you're surprised with what you find and how refreshed you feel. Slow down. Stroll. Enjoy the journey.

"Life is an ever-unfolding journey, with each new day granting us new opportunities. Don't forget to open your eyes, your mind, and your heart, to YOUR life."
~ Natalie Scott~

Gratitude

WHAT GIFT HAS THE WORLD GIVEN you today? Everyone has something to be happy about. Too often we just don't see it. We become accustomed to what's around us and are no longer aware of the goodness. Instead we focus on the annoyances, and we can even become too accepting of them.

Instead, develop a gratitude attitude to boost your happiness. Gratitude brings everything into balance, and gives you a proper perspective and appreciation for what you already have.

Begin your gratitude practice by being mindful of what's around you. Be present in the moment. Start with small things you are grateful for, those little magical moments. It can be as simple as your dog looking for a belly rub, twinkling fireflies, or a delicious fresh baked cookie.

Perhaps, a smile from a stranger. Try to find a few things that went well at work too, no matter how small.

Even look at something not so positive—and then flip to the other side of it. Like the electricity went out. Gee, now you have to sit by candlelight and just talk instead of watching TV. There's always something to be grateful for. Notice it daily, at random times throughout the day.

The process also involves facing the negative side of your life—divorce, job loss, bad boss—and finding the gratitude in them. It's not easy but it may provide you with an opportunity for learning or letting go. It will help you develop a new sense of strength and independence.

Once you regularly find the small things, you'll start noticing the big ones. Soon enough, you'll become more and more aware of your abundance. Just maybe, you'll find you are grateful for being in midlife. It surprised me one day not too long ago when I realized that indeed I was grateful for where I am in my life. I know myself far better than I ever did and I now have just what I want in my life.

Write little treasures in a journal, commonly called a Gratitude Journal. It doesn't have to be fancy. And it doesn't really matter how many things you find and write in a day, just so you find some. At the end of the week go back to your list and see all that you have in your life. When you're discouraged or stressed, and want something happy to cheer you up, just read your journal.

And remember to give more than you receive. Show gratitude to all who have helped you along the way.

*"When you are grateful, fear disappears
and abundance appears."*
~ Anthony Robbins ~

Happy

I USED TO THINK HAPPY was a light or silly aspiration. Now many organizations and studies have proven otherwise. One day a few years ago, deep into midlife, I realized I was feeling differently and wasn't sure what it was.

It dawned on me that I was very happy, a really full feeling of happiness. I was at peace in my life. That's not to say it was quiet and boring. I had a new wonderful romance. I was building a new career. My son was settled with a good job and a great girlfriend, now his wife. I was making more time for friends. My life was in balance, maybe for the first time. What a wonderful feeling.

Many years ago in my college yearbook, next to my senior picture I put this quote by Nathaniel Hawthorne, "Happiness is a butterfly, which when pursued, is always just beyond your grasp, but which, if you will sit down quietly, may alight upon you."

I hadn't thought about that quote until I was writing this. It surprises me in two ways. First, how "profound" I was at age 21 to pick that quote to represent me and second, that it took so many years to find true happiness. The transformation of my life to what it is today took a long time to get here. Don't let that be you.

What would happy look like for you? What dreams would make you happy? How will you reach them and live them? Now, go out and pursue them. At one point that elusive butterfly will alight upon your shoulder.

"Happiness is when what you think, what you say, and what you do are in harmony."
~ Mahatma Gandhi ~

I

AS IN "I NEED TO TAKE CARE OF MYSELF." If you're going to make things happen, you need to be in good all-around health. If you are stressed and miserable in mind and spirit, you are neglecting one important element of your success—you.

How are you taking care of yourself? Are you creating space just for you? Are you allowing yourself the time to discover the real you? Quiet time is needed to think, to dream, and let your ideas flow.

Especially in midlife, there are three main areas where your personal health affects your ability to move forward:

Mind: Your mind is your biggest asset. Ask yourself: What am I doing for inspiration? What do I watch, listen to, or read? Is it positive and nurturing, or negative and dis-empowering? Does it help me relax and open my mind? What can I do to nourish my mind?

Body: Taking care of our bodies too often falls to the bottom of our priority list. In midlife, you can't let that happen. You must honor your body. I'm not talking about looking youthful. I'm talking about energy. High energy will naturally create a more radiant inner glow and an outer beauty. It comes from regular exercise and healthy eating. You don't need me to tell you that. You just need the motivation. Remember your dream and your vision.

Spirit: What happens when you are depressed, worried, angry, or fearful? We experience a storm of emotions every day and way too many of them are negative. That's why it is important to make an extra effort to feed our spirit with positive words, thoughts, and motivators that uplift us in our journey. Find the source of positive energy that fuels you and add it to your daily and weekly routines. Try daily affirmations. When your spirits are high, it drives you to be your best self.

"Nothing is impossible;
the word itself says I'm possible."
~ Audrey Hepburn ~

Journal

TRACK YOUR MIDLIFE JOURNEY by keeping a journal. Document your awakening, what you are learning about yourself, your ideas of where you might want to head. Journaling is a powerful way to unleash your creativity, release blocks, and get past your inner critic. Later, you'll have a wonderful view of your journey (that's why it's called a journal!).

I strongly recommend that you get yourself a fabulous notebook or journal. One you'll enjoy picking up, one that represents you. Be sure you have a pen that easily flows. Nothing is more annoying than having your thoughts disrupted by something as silly as a scratchy pen.

Sounds old fashioned but there's something powerful about the hand written word. Just the act of writing down your thoughts, feelings, and dreams makes them more real. It slows you down. It helps you think and access your intuition.

Keeping a journal demonstrates to your inner self that you take this journey seriously. Writing helps you commit to your intentions. You hold yourself accountable. Once it's down on the page, a statement to yourself, you'll find more courage to act.

There is no wrong way to journal. Just start writing or drawing—whatever comes to mind. Allow a stream of consciousness to flow, releasing all of your mind chatter, even venting to release your negative energy.

Record the answers to the questions I've asked throughout this book. Be sure to include your feelings about answering tough questions, or how you feel about the progress, or lack of progress you are making. Even write about the reaction of those around you as you make your changes.

Let it flow naturally. It doesn't have to be a daily habit. Personally, I'm a random journaler. One thing's for sure; I'm always surprised reading my pages years later.

Tracking the progress of your journey helps you give credit to yourself. Acknowledgement develops your faith in your own inner powers. As you progress farther along your journey of growth and self-knowledge, it helps to see just how far you've come. Reflect and celebrate your accomplishments.

"The voyage of a journey is not in seeking new landscapes but in having new eyes."
~ Marcel Proust ~

Listen

TRUE LISTENING IS SOMETHING we so rarely do. In midlife, isn't it time we slow down a bit and take more in? There's no bigger gift you can give someone than being totally, fully present, and listening to what they are saying. It so rarely happens.

We don't often listen at a deep level. We are multi-taskers. If we're on the phone, most likely we're also checking email, especially if on a conference call for work. You're not fully engaged in any of the tasks you're doing. And if you're not, how can you be fully engaged in your job?

By not fully listening, the other person starts thinking she is not important to us. And at that moment she probably is not. We get caught up in our own feelings. We take things personally. We evaluate and judge what we're hearing.

How often do you simply say, "That's interesting, tell me more?" Instead, we tend to jump in with our own story or experience about whatever the person is going through. If it's a problem, they may just want to vent or talk out loud, and not need you to solve it or give advice. If it's a new idea, it may not be fully formed and you've just shot it down with why it won't work.

Mindful listening is allowing the other person to get her thoughts out without interrupting, not constantly looking for an opening. Just be present. She'll let you know what she needs from you. Or you can simply ask, after she finishes talking.

A good listener truly cares about the person talking. Keeping your attention on the other person will actually keep you interested. Stay in the moment. It's amazing. Be curious. Ask questions. Repeat back what you heard. Listening well will reduce misinterpretations which are often the center of arguments.

Let's get a bit closer – are you listening to your own life? Do you have a yearning you can't describe? Is your job draining you? Are you fearful of doing what you most desire to do? Shhhh! Listen to what your heart and soul are telling you. There is always a particular moment when you clearly know you need to change your life. You just need to be able to hear it.

Totally focused listening is one of the best gifts we can give anyone – family, friends or co-workers. Try it. Watch the other person's reaction. Who knows, maybe they will reciprocate.

"Our deepest wishes are
whispers of our authentic selves.
We must learn to respect them.
We must learn to listen."
~ Sarah Ban Breathnach ~

Knowledge

HOW WELL DO YOU really know yourself? To understand what I'm talking about, try this exercise. Off the top of your head, answer these three questions:

- o What unique gifts, talents and skills do I bring to this world?

- o What gives me meaning and purpose?

- o What makes me happy?

If you answered quickly and confidently, congratulations! You have an impressive degree of self-knowledge. And if you didn't, well, you're certainly not alone.

By midlife, you've built up a large knowledge base and skills from your job. What many of us don't have, even at this stage of life, is knowledge of ourselves. Midlife is the time when this painful realization happens and we begin an inward search for answers. It starts the inner exploration into knowing who you are—your strengths and weaknesses, what you want, what makes you happy, what you need to have in your life, and why you want it.

Building this authentic connection with who you are is part of the challenge of midlife, but really knowing yourself can guide you to make choices and decisions that truly match your sense of self.

"Knowing yourself is the beginning of all wisdom."
~ Aristotle ~

Meaningful

SO, HERE YOU ARE in midlife. You've been working for many years. Is it what you expected?

As we age into our 40s and 50s, we start asking "Is that all there is?" Something is missing. Maybe we've reached success but haven't gotten the satisfaction we expected to go with it. Or we've paid too big of a price in our personal life. Our goals shift. They become more expansive. They become more about how we relate to the bigger world around us. It's a shift from *how* as we build competency to the question of *why.*

A recent survey of midlife women conducted by More Magazine revealed some interesting (and not surprising) results. When asked to define the most important aspects of a great job, in addition to a good salary and benefits, 98% replied they needed more meaning—to feel that they're contributing positively.

It doesn't surprise me. I consistently hear this from my clients and other midlife women. We realize that some of our past goals had never been meaningful. We accepted them because society or our parents said they were important. We've followed a path we thought we should. Often, we just let our career move along without making conscious choices.

Each one of us creates our own definition of meaningful. Maybe you want to give back to society or put your skills to better use. Or just simply find a job that's a better fit to your values. One that lets that spark come back. One that you truly enjoy.

For some that means travelling a totally new path; for others it means finding a way to reconnect with their current career in a way that is more meaningful and more heart-centered. Try to identify the personally enriching things you can get from your current career—maybe opportunities to learn new things, travel, or work with people who inspire you. Perhaps you can look outside of work to find meaningful volunteer work or hobbies.

What does meaningful work mean to you? How would that manifest in your work? What makes you happy to go to work in the morning? What motivates you? Remember why you are working. You'll need this touchstone as you set out on the path of change.

"Your work is to discover your work and then with all your heart to give yourself to it."
~ Buddha ~

Network

BY MIDLIFE, WE USUALLY have a good network of trusting and supportive relationships. Do you go beyond it and also develop the broader more strategic network of mentors and associates?

Take a few minutes and assess the value of your support group and strategic connections:

- o Do you consciously take time to cultivate your relationships?

- o How often do you collaborate with someone outside your immediate team?

- o When was the last time you added people to your network?

- o How diverse is your network?

That last one is big. A rich blend of people can stretch your thinking and challenge assumptions.

These people can become crucial advisors and advocates.

Building a value network is about cultivating relationships that benefit both parties. It hinges on *giving*—not *taking*. The more you give freely, the more they will be there when you most need them. Share your knowledge and your connections. This viewpoint of abundance increases the exchange of advice, contacts, and moral support.

As you expand your network, think—what do you need from each person—and what can you offer in return? It might be an entrée into their network or introduction to another person who may be able to help. Be transparent and tell them directly what you need help with.

For a career changer, by far the biggest benefit of a solid network is finding the hidden job market. Often employers only broadcast an opening through people they know—their trusted sources. It's well documented that easily over half the vacancies are unpublicized and filled in this manner.

One of the best and easiest ways to extend your network is through LinkedIn, the professional networking tool. It helps turn a cold call introduction into a warm one. Be sure to create a complete profile that emphasizes and promotes your personal brand.

Even when requesting a LinkedIn introduction or connection, be on brand. You have only a few seconds to make a good impression. Introduce yourself by explaining the value you provide rather than your job title.

Be an authentic relationship-driven networker. Listen twice as much as you talk. Exude positive energy, smile—even if on the phone. Express interest in further conversations. Get to know people. Don't make contacts. Start relationships.

"You can do so little alone
and so much together."
~ Helen Keller ~

Obstacle

WHAT'S HOLDING YOU BACK? What obstacles are keeping you stuck? Even when we want to move forward there's always something stopping us. To overcome them, we need to figure out if it's an external obstacle or an internal block. Something external can be lessened or removed by taking action, no matter how small, to free the blockage. Internal may need more inner work.

To understand what's holding you back, quickly make a list of everything you feel is keeping you stuck. Keep going until everything is down. Don't edit it.

Look at each and ask: Is it true? If yes, examine your proof.

If it's real and tangible, it's probably an External Obstacle. Examples are lack of money, no time, don't have the skills, no support, or don't know what you want next. What small action step can be taken to remove it?

Or is it your *perceived* truth? These are inner blocks and broad beliefs you have about yourself. Do you hear yourself saying "I can't, I always, I never...?" They may include fear of failure, criticism, self-doubt, or fear of losing. These have become the rules of your life. Where did the belief come from? How true is it? How is it limiting you? What's another perspective?

A belief can be changed. Rather than reject it, be compassionate with yourself. Try to embrace it as "this is who I am now" and continue to work deeply to create your new reality.

Your beliefs are only interpretations. You can turn them around. Flip them over and make up positive versions. My yoga instructor always tells us "don't say you can't do it, because your mind and body will believe you." Even if your new positive version is not true yet, it will be soon enough.

Can't let it go? Here are a couple of fun ideas to help you shed them:

- o Bury it—literally. Write it out, put it in a box or envelope, dig a hole, and bury it.

- o Detach yourself by naming it as a character. Talk it down. "Now Josie, we're not thinking like that today."

- o Create a new rule, the opposite of how you feel. "As of today, I am ready to …"

Removing your obstacles will allow for synchronicity, recognizing, and taking hold of opportunity as it presents itself to you.

"Obstacles are those frightful things you see when you take your eyes off your goal."
~ Henry Ford ~

Path

TO PARAPHRASE THE CHESHIRE CAT "If you don't know where you are going, any path will do." Or this quote from Yogi Berra "If you don't know where you are going, you will wind up somewhere else."

That may be how many of us started on our current career and moved along without a conscious direction. Then we talked ourselves into staying for a variety of reasons. At this stage of midlife, that's no longer enough. It's time we find the path to our true authentic career.

How do you start down your new path? It's best to turn toward something positive, your vision for your life and career (see V), as opposed to turning away from something like the things you don't like about your job. You'll have more reason to stay focused and ignore distractions.

I always felt if I knew the endpoint I could put together a big detailed plan to get there the fastest way possible. But usually that proved overwhelming. Discouraged, I'd fall off the path.

What I found works better is with the end point in mind, choose a starting point. Include milestones or markers along the way. Even a short term path to keep paying the bills while in transition is a milestone as long as it's *consciously* part of the bigger vision.

And unexpected good things might happen. Not following a rigid path leaves room to explore opportunities that you could not have planned for when you started. Of course, they still need to be aligned with your end vision. Don't worry; now that you're in tune with yourself, you'll get warning signs if you move away from your values and priorities.

As you deepen your commitment to that end vision, build SMART goals. To make it manageable, break your long term milestones into smaller bits that can be integrated into your daily short term plan.

Celebrating every one of those smaller accomplishments will keep you motivated. It brings your future into the present little by little.

"Do not go where the path may lead;
go instead where there is no path
and leave a trail."
~ Ralph Waldo Emerson ~

Questions

AT NO OTHER STAGE in our life do we have as many questions. Too often though, they just swirl around inside our head. A systematic way of asking questions and processing your answers will help lead you to someplace new. Asking ourselves focused questions causes us to think, create answers we believe in, and motivates us to act.

The root word of question is quest—a journey seeking something important. At this time of midlife—that's YOU—who you truly are and how to live a life that reflects that.

The best and somewhat obvious questions are the tried and true "Who, What, Where, When and How." I caution adding "Why" as it's too often used as recrimination as in "Why did you do this and not that?" We get defensive, causing self-doubt to raise its ugly head. A better way is to ask "Why" after each of the other questions and keep asking it until you uncover and deeply understand your motivation.

When I work with clients, I have a specific order and approach that I use to ask questions – helping them draw out the answers almost without realizing it. It's like pulling a thread to unravel the secret of who you are.

Nobody knows more about you than you. These are your skills and talents, your values, your experience, your expertise. You are the resident expert on you. The key to change is less about knowing exactly *what* to do than being *motivated* to do it. We are more motivated to carry out our own ideas and solutions than being told what to do. We've already been there, done that.

Try this exercise to uncover your motivation. Continue with the questions above. Get out your journal. Think of where you are right now in your life, in your career. Start with "What." What are your top three challenges? What's missing in your life? What is the biggest change you want to make right now? What's motivating you right now? What's holding you back?

Work your way through the other "W's" toward perhaps the most essential question, the one that everything else is based on. Throughout all your highs and lows, the answer to this question will keep you grounded: "Who do you want to be?"

"Tell me, what is it you plan to do with your one wild and precious life?"
~ Mary Oliver ~

Restless

I STARTED PICKING MY R WORD around "re" words like reinvention, renewal, realign but realized under all that was "restless." Restlessness is a hallmark of midlife. It's the urge to make a fresh start. We have an unnamed longing for something more.

It's a time for evaluation, perhaps triggered by a major life event—the loss of a job, a divorce, an empty nest, a milestone birthday, a health crisis, or the death of a parent. We are stopped in our tracks, and forced to reevaluate where we are, and where we want to be. Feelings of regret and failure are not uncommon. You have a sense of having lost your way. What to do about it? How do you want to spend the rest of your life?

Millions of midlife women begin feeling restless in their careers. At this midpoint of life, your career may have left you bored, empty, or quite often worn out. Some women can renew themselves while staying in the same job or field. Many others use their skills in an entirely new way. And many take the plunge of starting their own businesses for the first time. It's not surprising that the majority of female-owned companies are run by women in midlife.

Studies show that up to 80 percent of baby boomers plan to do some sort of paid work until age 70 to stay mentally sharp, socially engaged, and financially secure. We're all pioneers in this new longevity revolution. Can you re-energize or do you reinvent your career? Oops, more R's.

Often this time around, you want to do something different, but you haven't got a clue. Successful career transitions don't happen by accident. Listen to your restless heart and mind. What is it telling you? What is it drawing you toward?

"When we tire
of well-worn ways, we seek for new.
This restless craving in the souls of men
spurs them to climb,
and to seek the mountain view."
~ Ella Wheeler Wilcox ~

Story

YOUR PERSONAL BRAND comes through your stories—where you've been, who you are, and what's made you who you are today. It's important to clearly articulate your story. Even more important than telling the story, is owning your story.

By owning, it I mean really standing in it. Liking it. Every inch of it. The good and the not so good. It sounds easier than it is which is why most of us don't do it.

We trivialize our achievements. We ignore what others see as assets. We think our stories aren't interesting enough. We compare our stories and see ourselves falling short. We don't see our own value.

When you start to embrace and own the place you are in right now—the story of your life and career—your authentic self takes over, leading to more courage and confidence.

So how do you own your story? You learn to like it.

Learn to see all the steps that got you to where you are today as having purpose and value. Think of it as your evolution. Step back and look at yourself objectively as if you are someone you have never met telling your story. Are you interested in what she's saying?

Spend time with a pen and paper writing down all those things you're good at, have experience with, the places you've lived, the adventures you've embarked on, the mark you want to make on the world, what makes you smile. This is what makes you unique.

The one thing you have that nobody else has is your voice, your mind, your story, your vision. The more you allow yourself to believe that your story matters, the more you own it. Package it as part of your personal branding so you can confidently explain your value and contribution, especially in your resume and your introductions while networking. It helps the listener to see the whole you. Most people can't do this. You will jump ahead of your competition.

Midlife may be the time to write the next chapter of your story, but first you have to own today's story.

"If you keep telling the same sad small story,
you will keep living the same sad small life."
~ Jean Houston ~

Transition

WE OFTEN MIX UP the use of transition and change. But they are very different. Change is a situation that happens in our life—getting laid off, fired, married, divorced, and yes, menopause. Transition on the other hand, is the psychological shift and personal development we go through to adapt to those changes, to make them work. Change can happen in an instant, whereas transition is a process.

You're ready for a new job. Either your current one has run its course and is no longer a fit, or maybe you've been laid off, or fired. One is your choice, the other is not. The simplest route is to go out and look for a similar job. The problem with this direction is you will bring the same problems and issues with you.

In midlife, the better course is to pause and allow yourself to go through the transition stages William Bridges, life-change specialist and author of *Transitions: Making Sense of Life's Changes*, says we need to work through for personal growth. First is an ending of the old—letting go, clearing out the junk and baggage. Next, moving into the neutral zone may be confusing and uncomfortable at first. But as you learn more about yourself through inquiry and exploration you come to realize you are transforming into the person you need to be to move forward into the third stage—the beginning of your next chapter.

The dragonfly, the icon of my coaching business, is a symbol of transition. More than half of its life is lived in water until it's time to rise above into the air. Eventually, gathering what it needs to transform, it climbs out of the water, transitioning into a creature of the wind and light. As dragonflies mature, their colors become more vibrant, revealing their deepest inner beauty.

As creatures of water they are said to symbolize the subconscious or the dreaming mind. They ask us to pay more attention and be aware of our deepest thoughts and desires. They remind us to let our own inner light shine through with a new vision, to achieve balance with mental clarity, to go past self-created limitations to stretch and grow. They symbolize the sense of self that comes with maturity.

Have you been living under water? Take inspiration from the dragonfly.

Dragonfly
Gossamer faerie
Iridescent inner light
Change, transform, renew
~ Diane Topkis ~

Unique

YOU ARE UNIQUE. Just as no two snowflakes are alike, you are like no one else. You are the only one who has your unique combination of skills, talents, and values. Your experience and your perspective on it, is your very own. This is your career value. Learn to appreciate and celebrate your uniqueness. Come to own it as the wonderful distinctiveness that it offers you.

Your uniqueness is tied to your potential and who you can become. Understanding what you excel at, what you're passionate about makes it easier to identify the places you belong, the people who will appreciate you and the professions where you can blossom.

How you define and achieve success both in your life and career is different than anyone else. By midlife, I'm sure that you've had successes as well as failures. It's also likely that they were someone else's or at least your younger definition of what success should be.

When my clients ask the question: "Where do you think I can find career success?" I explain that's the wrong question. You'll find success when you can answer "How can I translate my unique value into today's labor market?"

What is your unique equation for success? This is a special formula that's yours alone. Learn to use it well and you will find your success. Go back and read about your personal brand—how to define and package the uniqueness of what you offer the world. Once you put that together, nothing can stop you.

"You do not merely want to be considered just the best of the best. You want to be considered the only one who does what you do."
~ Jerry Garcia ~

Vision

REAL CHANGE BEGINS when you have clear dreams and a vision of yourself living a life full of passion and purpose. It's a vision of what gives your life meaning and passion based on your definition of success.

Having a compelling vision gets you excited and motivated about your goals. It makes them more real and tangible. It pulls you forward and propels you into action to take steps to create this life. If you feel discouraged and your motivation lags, you can come back to the vision and be renewed in your energy to work towards your goals.

The mystery of the law of attraction is that all your thoughts, all images in your mind, and all the feelings connected to your thoughts will later manifest as your reality. Your level of conscious focus, determines what you attract into your life. When we set a vivid vision with positive emotions in our mind, synchronicity often follows. We find ourselves encountering the necessary opportunities to reach our vision.

The problem is that usually we know what we *don't* want and have difficulty expressing what we *do* want. Since you receive the type of energy you send out, if you only focus on what you don't want, unfortunately that's what you'll continue to get.

So we start by dreaming to allow your vision to become clear. Find a quiet peaceful place. Try a few key questions to prime your dream pump. Free yourself. Dream big.

- o What are you most passionate about?

- o What do you have the most energy for?

- o What accomplishments or legacy would have the ultimate significance for you?

- o If you had unlimited resources and could not fail, what would you do?

- o Imagine you're 80 years old, which dream causes you the greatest regret for NOT pursuing?

o   What causes you the greatest happiness?

When you are ready to bring your dream into the open, create a vision board—an intuitive selection of powerful, meaningful images that will bring your vision to life and boost your ability to believe in it. It's a magical energy exercise especially when coupled with a vivid, emotionally filled description. The last step ties it to your day to day life. Write an aspirational mission statement to guide you on your path to your next chapter. Keep these visible. Reference them often.

These complimentary tools are powerful. Look for a future book in my Career Clarity Series on how they can work for you. You have unlimited potential to make any dream come true.

"Whatever the mind can conceive
and believe, it can achieve."
~ Napolean Hill ~

Who

WHO ARE YOU and what do you stand for? This is the most important step in bringing clarity to your midlife, especially in making a career transition. That, in turn, determines what you do and how you do it. Too often it's the job that has defined who we are. That needs to change in midlife.

Your personal success formula is connecting your inner purpose and passion (who you are) with your outer strategies and goals (what you do and how you do it). It all starts with self-exploration to fully understand your unique values, talents, gifts, and skills.

Once this is clear, write an aspirational mission statement about who you want to be—what you see for yourself in an ideal world, based on your values. It will give power to the intention of how you want to live your life. Consider it a guide for your path of life.

It's less about what you want to accomplish and more what you *believe in*—the ethics, morals, and values that you want to govern your life and career. It's a way to actively focus your energy, actions, and behavior. It helps you make decisions in your day to day life based on your core values and beliefs.

When you are in a complex, confusing, or emotional situation, use the mission words to help guide you to the right decision. Does it fit with *who I want to be* in the world? How can I respond that keeps me aligned with my mission in life?

Decisions may still be complex but by using your mission statement as guidance, at least you know you are staying true to who you are. I know mine has helped me tremendously in relationships, especially with my family. In time, I've found my sibling relationships much more loving.

Writing a clear aspirational mission statement needs deep self-inquiry to answer these questions, especially the first one:

- o   Who do I want to be as a person?
- o   What value do I create?
- o   Who do I help?
- o   How do I accomplish it?
- o   How do I live my life?

Keep it in your wallet. Post it on a wall. Read it every day to remind you of who you are and who you want to be.

*"It is not the question, what am I going
to be when I grow up;
you should ask the question,
who am I going to be when I grow up."*
~ Goldie Hawn ~

eXperience

I KNOW THIS IS CHEATING a little but I don't hear the "e," do you? By midlife, you have quite a bit of life experience, some good and some not so good. No matter which, they are what make you, you. Acknowledge and accept them all.

Your experience must be fully tapped to understand where you are headed. There is no such thing as waste in your life and career. Every experience, good or bad, can be leveraged into your destiny. The key is finding the meaning in the pain or difficulty, and to understand that every experience is a qualification.

What has your life prepared you to do? What experiences have most shaped you as a person? How have these experiences prepared you for what you want to do in life and career? Compare experiences across all parts of your life—from childhood to midlife. Even a big reinvention will be built from your experiences.

Of course, your experience includes the skills and knowledge acquired at work. What do others come to you for that you do in a unique way that almost no one else can? How can you incorporate those into something more meaningful?

Don't forget to dig into your failures as part of your experience. They too are steps in your journey. What lessons have they taught you? Think of the entrepreneurs who believe they haven't tried hard enough or pushed the boundaries if they haven't failed at least once and sometimes the bigger the failure, the bigger the badge of honor, the bigger the lessons. Sometimes, failing brings you credibility that others don't have. It's all how you frame it, especially in your own mind.

It's up to you to find the spark you gained from your life experiences, and let it shine through.

"Experience is not what happens to a man.
It is what a man does with what happens to him."
~ Aldous Huxley ~

ıg

AUTHENTIC YOU.

ırolonged, strong

t fits midlife. One

uch. If you say it

feels like a song,

...ₒ ...aι ıııldlife feeling:

- ○ It's the feeling that something is missing.

- ○ It's a realization that life is somehow falling short.

- ○ It's the desire for something more authentic.
- ○
- ○ It's knowing that it's time for change.

- ○ It's time to make different, more conscious choices.

o It's time for more meaning and purpose in our life.

Yearning – what a powerful word!

"My dad used to draw these great cartoon figures.
His dream was being a cartoonist,
but he never achieved it,
and it kind of broke my heart.
I think part of my interest in art had to do with
his yearning for something he could never have."
~Kathryn Bigelow ~

Zest

YOU HAVE IT! Midlife women have an amazing vitality and zest for life. Maybe it's the urgency that there's so much yet to do. Or maybe it's shaking off some old roles and attitudes.

Whatever it is, I have met more midlife women who have a real passion, curiosity, and desire to learn, explore, and experience.

Various dictionaries describe zest as making something more stimulating and enjoyable, an exciting or interesting aspect of something that makes it particularly enjoyable. That's you at midlife. What some may consider baggage is what makes you so interesting. It's your story. It's who you are and what made you, you.

What midlife crisis? This age is about opportunity—to really understand ourselves—

what matters to us, what's important, and what makes us happy. And making conscious choices to act on it—to go get it—and to do it with gusto.

That includes going for the midlife career shift, whether bettering ourselves in our current job or looking for a different, more authentic one. This is the time to learn new skills, start new ventures, whatever it takes to rekindle the spark for your work and life.

It's time to let your potential blossom in what I read someplace described as the *"most golden, most extraordinary, and luminous"* phase of a woman's life. You know how the zest of a lemon or lime perks up the taste of everything. Well, you are the zest of your own midlife!

*"Zest is the secret of all beauty.
There is no beauty that is attractive without zest."*
~ Christian Dior ~

What do I do next?

WE COVERED 26 KEYS to help you gain the clarity and confidence to make a midlife career transition. I posed many questions throughout. The first step of this journey is to understand who and where you are – and then determine what kind of change needs to be made.

Many people contemplate job changes after a particularly bad day or week at work. However, the decision to change career paths shouldn't be a quick one. And it may not even need to be a complete change. Can you re-energize the job you currently have?

Take the following steps. Focus on meaning, not money. Look for what you need that will bring fulfillment to your work.

I hope this is a start of a conversation—with me as an author and coach but most importantly, a conversation and inquiry with yourself.

Action Items

1. Go back and review the 26 keys. Some are geared for action and some just provide a deeper understanding of what's necessary to make a midlife transition.

2. Which ones jumped out at you as needing your focus?

3. Pull out a journal and pick several to work on.

4. Ask: How am I doing in this area? Answer the posed questions. Dig deep for true answers.

5. Look for creative ways to improve. Set goals, even just baby steps to move forward.

6. If you would like a more structured approach, take a look at my career coaching programs at www.YourNextChapterNOW.com.

Thank you for reading

I HOPE YOU ENJOYED reading this book, the first in my Career Clarity series. I also hope you uncovered some answers and ideas on how to make a successful midlife career transition. Or maybe the reading gave you many more questions. Either way, I hope it started your move forward.

I'd love to hear from you on how the book helped, or suggestions for what is missing, and what struggles you are facing in your career. You can contact me on my website at www.YourNextChapterNOW.com.

Do you think this book can help others in a similar situation as yours? I'd be very grateful if you could leave a short review of the book on Amazon. It will help other midlife women who are stuck and uncertain about changing careers. And it will help me improve this and future books in my series.

Please share this book with your network of friends through your favorite social media channels.

Many thanks for spending time with me!

Meet the Coach

AS THE MIDLIFE WOMAN'S CAREER COACH, I love helping midlife women (and enlightened men) gain the clarity and confidence to reinvent or re-energize their career into meaningful work for their next chapter. My clients have successfully discovered new possibilities and developed new levels of personal and professional success.

I designed my CLEAR Path signature coaching program specifically for midlife women to guide them to their desired outcomes in the shortest amount of time. It's an integrated model of coaching, exploring many aspects of their life as well as career. The process works through every step of their change process from self-discovery through transition into their new career.

My Story: From Boiled Frog to Life I Love

I'M A CAREER COACH who works with midlife women who have reached a turning point, ready to make a significant career change but not sure how or even what to do. Sometimes we're stuck in the same routine, living life by default. It's easy to just stay there until something breaks and knocks you out off track—whether you're ready or not. I know that's what happened to me.

My rut may have been grooved as a reaction to too much change when I was young, attending nine different school systems. I vowed when older, I'd stay put. I wasn't wild about the college I chose to get my degree in education and psychology but stayed so I wouldn't be the new girl in school yet again. Then I fell into my career with a large company when teaching jobs were non-existent. I stayed for over 35 years, having a variety of jobs in sales and marketing. Along the way I got married and although the relationship changed in the later years, stayed for over 25 years. Catching a pattern?

I was the story of the boiled frog. In high school biology, I learned if you put a frog into a beaker of cool water and slowly bring the temperature up, it will adapt until it finally dies when the boiling point is reached. Although those early years made me adverse to change, I also became very adaptive, making the best of situations. Luckily, I jumped out of that beaker when I hit midlife!

Typical midlife reflection of "where am I in my life?" turned into an opportunity to make some major life changes—some planned and some not. My last years have been all about transitions. As my son neared college graduation (empty nest), I decided to end my marriage (divorce).

As for my career, I know I had plateaued. I stopped making huge efforts. The bureaucracy wore me down or so I tell myself. I toyed with leaving but decided to stay for just a few more years and retire to do what I've always wanted, whatever that was. But my company had different ideas. I was caught in a "resource action" (laid off). I was shocked. How could they do this to me? I was still a top performer. I was a team leader—coaching and mentoring many on my team. How could they get along without me?

After the shock, anger, and grieving for my job passed, I realized this was my turning point. I accepted what a fellow coach calls, my "free agent" pass. I quickly discarded pursuing the same type of job. Time for something new. Time to find a more purposeful career. But what?

In came Cheryl, my outplacement counselor, who quickly became my career coach. She had me explore my values, what I enjoyed, did well, and helped me brainstorm how to put it to use. I started observing what my coach was doing—supporting, encouraging, asking questions. She was pulling stuff out of me I had never fully explored.

A light bulb flashed on. I wanted to help others like me, midlife women, find their way. I was excited. It felt right. My inner voice was driving me to my natural talents. It was an extension of what I've always done both professionally and personally—helping colleagues and friends find clarity, see a path, and encouraging them to realize their potential.

Now, I love what I do. I have a very rewarding career, one that includes a deep sense of peace, freedom, joy, and fulfillment. As a coach and author, I get to help midlife women like you gain the clarity and confidence to reinvent or re-energize their career into meaningful work for their next chapter.

Does any of this sound familiar to your situations? If this book has inspired you to take the next step to build a career you love—and to get someone to hold you accountable, I'd be honored to help.

To sign-up for my blog updates and learn more about how we can work together, please go to www.YourNextChapterNOW.com.

Books by Diane Howell Topkis

Career Clarity Series

Love It or Leave It: Is it time to change your career?

WRITTEN FOR MIDLIFE WOMEN who hate their job but not sure what to do about it, this book is focused on solving that concern/problem—how to decide if you can reenergize your current career enough to love it—or do you need to leave it and reinvent your skills into a completely new direction. In this ebook, you'll find a link to download a free workbook to write out your answers to questions posed.

The following is from *Love It or Leave It.*

Your Personal Definition of Success

A career transition can be defined as conducting a search of yourself in order to move forward towards work that is more compatible with who you are. These are the typical elements of a satisfying career:

- o Uses your strengths
- o Challenges you
- o Is meaningful to you
- o Matches your values and personality
- o Fits into your life and future you envision

Most of us have never taken the time to define what success means—besides the obvious one about advancement and salary levels. For what purpose and reasons are you working? Did you make conscious choices regarding your career path?

One of the most important career and life-planning activities you can engage in is finding your own definition of success. If you haven't done this, how do you know what's best for you?

How can you make career decisions if you aren't crystal clear about how you define success? How can you be happy if you don't know when you're successful?

Even if you haven't taken the time to define success, success has already been defined for you. Perhaps unknowingly, you've already followed models of career and life success. The question is whether they were your own or ones you inherited from family or society.

This current model of success may or may not work for you. If you follow a path to success that isn't your own, you may achieve your goals, but when you arrive at your destination, you may not feel successful or fulfilled.

Until you understand exactly what success means to YOU, no change will bring you satisfaction. It may alleviate your current pain but not for long. Take an initial look at what makes you happy. You can refine it later. You can even have several definitions as long as they don't contradict each other. Complete this sentence:

I know I'm successful when...

▶
▶
▶

Now you need to understand why this is important to you. Keep asking yourself "why?" and "is this what I *really* want?" until it rings true.

Available on Amazon.com.

A Girl's Gotta Have Fun

I'VE OFTEN COACHED and written about the importance of adding activities that you're passionate about to your life beyond your career.

I love visiting wine regions on vacation. It takes us to beautiful, picturesque parts of the country and world. We've traveled to the Chianti region of Italy and in the US to Virginia, Oregon, the Finger Lakes, the east end of Long Island, and Paso Robles to name a few and then built a vacation around wine tasting.

We have visited so many over the years, I tend to forget some of the places and the wines tasted. So I decided to take my passion for writing in a new direction.

I created a different kind of wine journal. One that I could not find anywhere. One that focuses on traveling and exploring wineries in a region. I researched and included a reference section including a Flavor and Aroma Guide and the Etiquette of Tasting.

The *Wine Tasting Journal* was so much fun to write, I decided to write a tasting series. I've added a *Craft Spirit Tasting Journal* and *Craft Beer Tasting Journal.*

All journals are available on Amazon and Barnes & Noble.

Made in the
USA
Monee, IL

15193965R30059